STRUMMING THE GUITAR
BY RON CENTOLA

To Jennifer
and
Mark

Edited by Anna H. Centola and Gary Centola

TABLE OF CONTENTS

LIST OF SONGS (RHYTHMS)

INTRODUCTION

This book is intended for the guitarist of all ages. It provides a step by step method for learning how to strum your guitar and how to change easily from one chord to another.

There are special sections at the end of the book to help you in learning how to use a capo and to aid you in creating your own strums on the guitar.

I hope that strumming and chording will be made easy and pleasurable by the new approaches in this book.

Ron Centola

SPECIAL FEATURES

1) Important points to remember are in bold print.

2) Instructions are set out in step by step form.

3) A method is set forth enabling you to develop your skills from playing easy chords and strums to creating more advanced chording and strumming.

4) You are not only shown chord positions but how to move your fingers from one chord to another in a smooth flowing manner.

5) There is a special section on how to use a capo.

6) Instructions are given helping you to learn how to create your own strum patterns.

STRUMMING BROKEN INTO FOUR SIMPLE RULES

Learning how to strum is broken down into the four steps listed below. In the following pages each step will be explained and practiced in great detail.

Step 1

You will learn the finger positions of the chords needed for a song. The left hand is used for the fingering of chord positions on the neck of the guitar.

Step 2

You will then learn how to change from one chord to another.

Step 3

You will be able to use your strumming hand (right hand) so that you will be able to play the strum smoothly without breaking the strum. (A strum pattern is the way your hand moves up and down across the strings).

Step 4

Finally, you will learn how to sing and concentrate on the words of a song while keeping your strumming at an even smooth pace. In order to be successful at step number four, you must be able to do what you have learned in the above three steps without looking at your right or left hands. (You can't look at your hands and watch the words and chords to a song at the same time).

THE THREE BEGINNING CHORDS

Step 1

You must learn the finger positions of the chords needed for a song.

The A Seventh (A7) Chord

To play **A⁷** you put your **1st finger** on the **2nd fret** of the **4th string**. You put your **2nd finger** on the **2nd fret** of the **2nd string**.

A⁷ (The Right Way)   **A⁷**   **A⁷** (The Wrong Way)

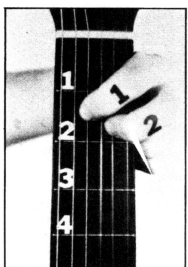   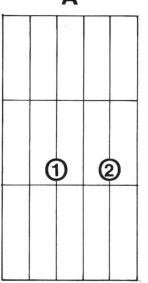   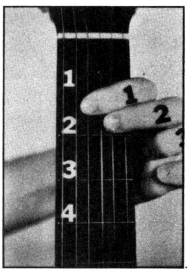

Your **fingers should be up straight** as in this photo. The more you turn your wrist counter-clock wise the straighter your fingers will become.

If you allow your fingers to lay or press down on other strings, your chord will not have a clear sound.

In conclusion your fingers should only press or touch the strings that are indicated on the diagram. (**Your 1st finger** in the above **A⁷** chord should **only be touching or pressing** on the **4th string, 2nd fret.** Your **2nd finger** should **only be touching or pressing** on the **2nd string, 2nd fret.**

The A Chord

To play **A** you put your **1st finger** on the **2nd fret** of the **4th string.** You put your **2nd finger** on the **2nd fret** of the **3rd string.** You put your **third finger** on the **2nd fret** of the **2nd string.**

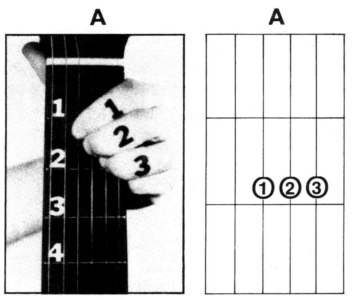

The D Chord

To play **D** you put your **1st finger** on the **2nd fret** of the **3rd string.** You put your **2nd finger** on the **2nd fret** of the **1st string.** You put your **3rd finger** on the **3rd fret** of the **2nd string.**

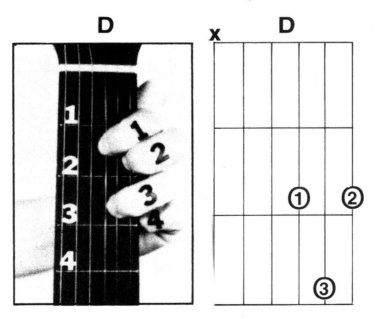

Step 1 - Learn the finger positions for these 3 chords before before continuing on. ☐

CHANGING CHORDS

Step 2

You should be able to change from one chord to another without any hesitation.

Flow Charts

The **flow chart** provides a **means of showing you** how to **move from one chord to another with as little effort as possible.** The less you move your fingers around, the more smoothly and quickly you will be able to change from one chord to another.

Changing From D To A⁷

By means of arrows these diagrams show the movement of your fingers while changing from a **D** to an **A⁷** chord. There is no arrow on finger 3 because it is not needed in the **A⁷** chord.

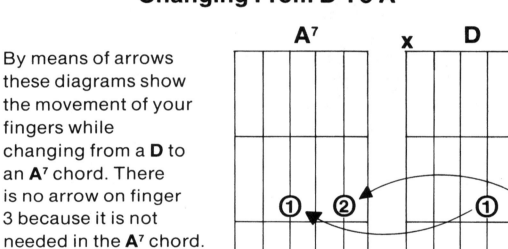

The above diagrams demonstrate how when changing from a **D** to an **A⁷** you must **move your 1st finger from** the **2nd fret of the 3rd string to** the **2nd fret of the 4th string** while **moving your 2nd finger from** the **2nd fret of the 1st string to the 2nd fret of the 2nd string. At the same time pick up** your **3rd finger** because it is not needed in the **A⁷** chord.

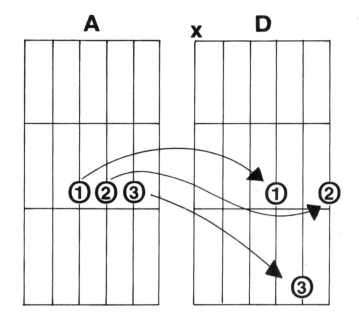

To change from **A** to **D, move** your **1st finger from** the **2nd fret of the 4th string to** the **2nd fret** of the **3rd string while moving** your **2nd finger from the 2nd fret** of the **3rd string** to the **2nd fret of the 1st string. At the same time, move** your **3rd finger from** the **2nd fret** of the **2nd string** to the **3rd fret of** the **2nd string.**

Conclusion

1) The above example shows you the most efficient way of moving your fingers from one chord to another. Hopefully, this and other examples of finger movement will help you find your own easiest and shortest way of changing from one chord to another.

2) You'll get plenty of practice using these chords on the following pages.

If you can change from a **D** to **A** to **A⁷** without any hesitation, you have completed **Step 2.** □

STRUMMING

Step 3

You will be able to use your strumming hand (right hand) so that you will be able to play the strum smoothly without breaking the strum pattern.

Straight Down Strum

1) A straight down strum is indicated by the following symbol (⊓).

2) You must **brush across the strings** of the guitar **evenly. Do not hit one string at a time.**

3) When changing from one chord to another, **do not stop moving your strumming hand.**

4) With a straight down strum just strike the strings with the down swing of your wrist. On the up swing of your wrist you do not strike the strings.

5) Most of the work of **strumming** should be done with your wrist and not your arm. **Think of shaking a thermometer. You should keep your arm and wrist relaxed.** If your arm is tired after strumming a song, you are using too much arm and not enough wrist.

6) Try to make each strum sound like it is running together with the following strum so you get one complete, even sound.

7) Try the helpful tips on the next page.

Using The D Chord

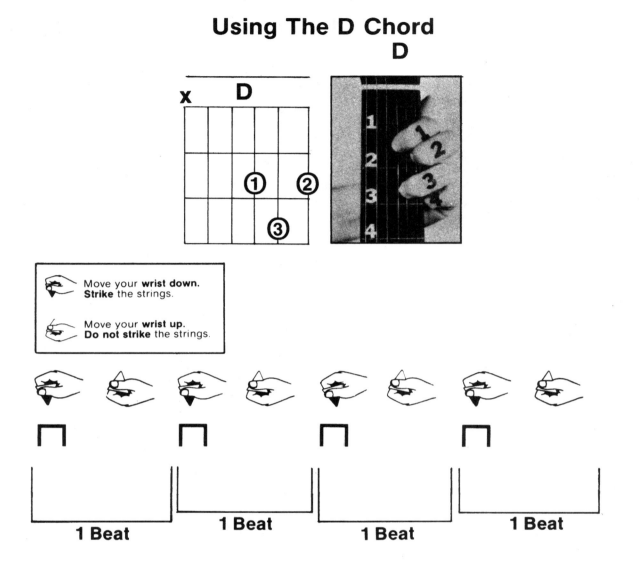

1) Above is a straight down strum for a 4 beat time span.

2) On the down swing of your wrist you should strike the **D** chord.

3) On the up swing of your wrist you do not strike the strings.

4) For ease of understanding at this point, we will consider **one beat as the time it takes** to **strike** the **strings on a down swing and bring your hand up on the up swing of your wrist.**

Foot Tapping Test

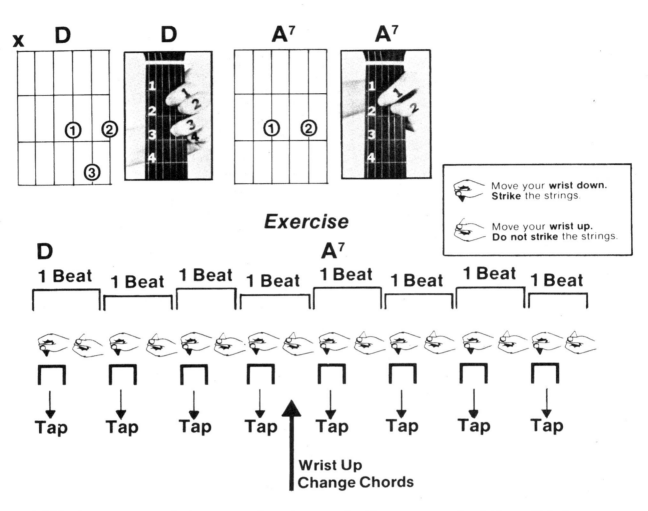

1) We have stated that one beat equals the amount of time it takes your strumming hand to go down and up again.

2) **A beat is measured as the time between each tap of the foot. The taps should be evenly spaced and simultaneous with the strum.**

3) As you tap your foot, each strum should accompany the tap of your foot on the floor.

4) On the up swing of your wrist you should change from the **D** to the **A⁷** chord. This should be done without stopping the tap or the strum.

5) **You should be able to play the above exercise within 8 taps or 8 beats.**

Strum Pattern - Down Up (⊓V)

1) The symbol for striking the strings on the down swing of your wrist is indicated by the following symbol. (⊓).

2) The symbol for striking the strings on the upswing of your wrist is indicated by the following symbol (**V**).

3) The first strum pattern we will try is
⊓V⊓V⊓V⊓V (down up down up down up down up

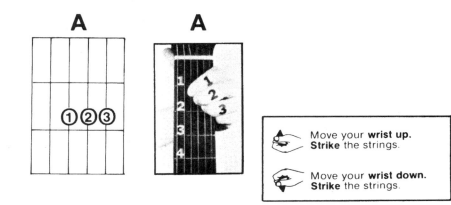

Down Up (⊓V) Strum Pattern

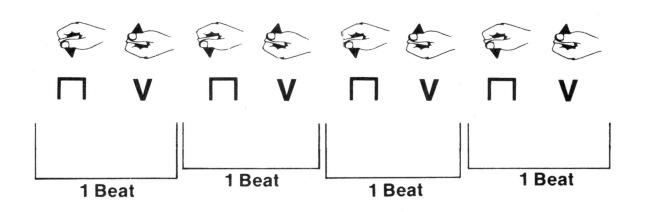

1) **You strike the A** on the down and the up swing of your wrist.

2) **Striking the A on the down and the up swing of your wrist is one beat.**

Foot Tapping Test

Use The A Chord

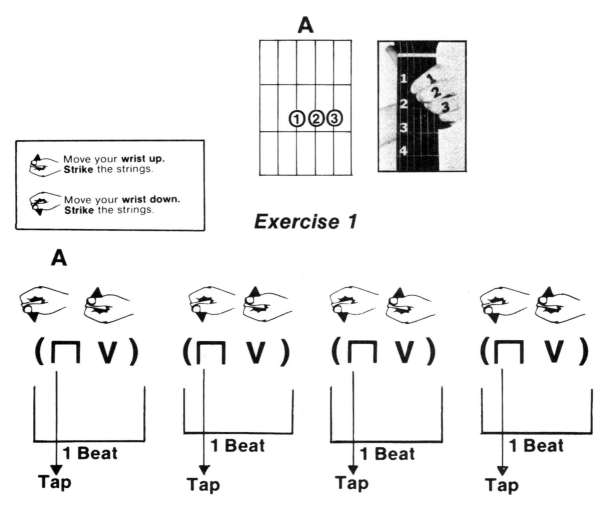

A

Move your **wrist up.**
Strike the strings.

Move your **wrist down.**
Strike the strings.

Exercise 1

A

(⊓ V) (⊓ V) (⊓ V) (⊓ V)

1 Beat   1 Beat   1 Beat   1 Beat

Tap   Tap   Tap   Tap

1) Each ⊓ V is one beat. A beat is the amount of time it takes your foot to go down and up.

2) Your down strum would occur as your foot taps the floor and your up strum as your foot is being brought back up again.

3) The **above exercise** should be **played** in the **amount of time** it **takes** your **foot** to **strike the floor 4 times** or 4 beats.

Strum Pattern - Down Up (⊓V)

(Exercise)

It is very important that you can change chords without breaking the strum pattern. Below is an example of how to do that. You will get much more practice using this strum pattern when you play the songs that follow this exercise.

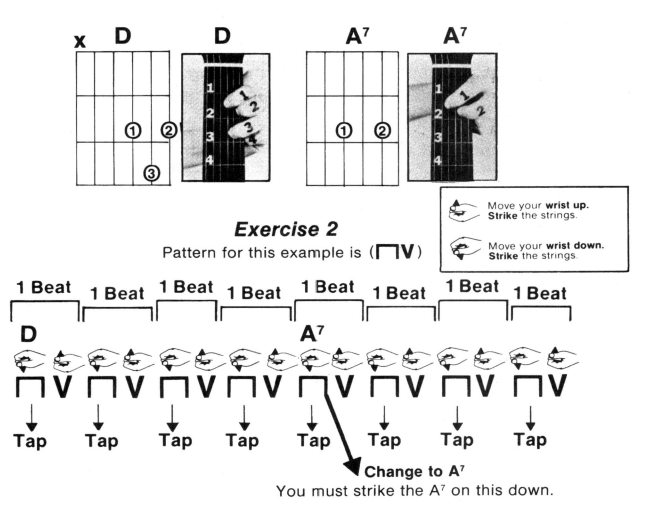

Exercise 2

Pattern for this example is (⊓V)

Move your **wrist up.**
Strike the strings.

Move your **wrist down.**
Strike the strings.

1 Beat **1 Beat** **1 Beat** **1 Beat** **1 Beat** **1 Beat** **1 Beat** **1 Beat**

D ⊓V ⊓V ⊓V ⊓V **A⁷** ⊓V ⊓V ⊓V ⊓V

Tap Tap Tap Tap Tap Tap Tap Tap

Change to A⁷
You must strike the A⁷ on this down.

1) **You should be able to play this exercise within 8 beats or 8 taps of your foot.**

2) Your foot and your strumming hand should not stop moving during the 8 beats.

3) Your strumming pattern should not be broken during the exercise.

4) If you can play the above strum without breaking the strum pattern, you have completed **Step 3.** ☐

ACTUAL PLAY OF SONGS (1)

Here is an opportunity for you to bring all that you have learned into the playing and strumming of songs. If you can play the following songs without breaking your strumming pattern, you have completed **Step 4.**

Two Strum Patterns For Each Song

1) The songs have only the words and chords marked in.

2) You must sing the tunes and play the chords while singing. (It doesn't matter how your voice sounds. You are doing this to practice your strumming.)

3) You should **first play** the song with the **straight down strum, changing chords** when **you see** the **chord change** on **top of the words.**

4) You **don't** have to **worry** about **how many times to strike the chord.** Your **only concern** should be in **changing from one chord to another without stopping.**

5) **Once** you can **play** the **entire song** with the **straight down strum, play the song** with **the ⊓V strum pattern.**

6) When playing the ⊓V strum pattern you should strike each chord ⊓V ⊓V until you see the change of chord on top of the words.

7) You don't have to worry how many times to strike each chord ⊓V. Your only concern should be to keep the strum pattern going throughout the song and chord changes.

HE'S GOT THE WHOLE WORLD IN HIS HANDS

D ⇨   *A⁷* ⇨
He's got the whole world in His hands, He's got the whole world

                    D ⇨
in His hands, He's got the whole world in His hands, He's got the

A⁷ ⇨   *D* ⇨
whole world in His hands. He's got you and me brother, in His hands,

        A⁷ ⇨   *D* ⇨
He's got you and me sister, in His hands, He's got you and me

                        A⁷ ⇨   *D* ⇨
brother, in His hands, He's got the whole world in His hands.

Helpful Advice

1) Try to concentrate on singing the words and **changing chords smoothly without breaking your strum pattern.** Remember, all you have to do is change the chords when you see them above the words you are singing.

2) Remember, try the **strum pattern (⊓V) only after** you can **play** the **song through** with the **straight strum.**

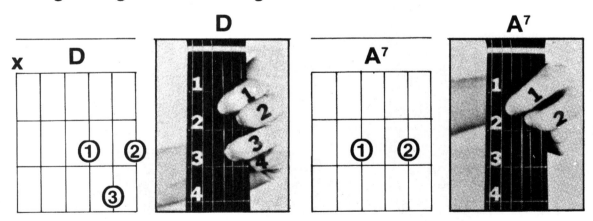

CLEMENTINE

D⇨   **A⁷**⇨
In a cav - ern, in a can - yon, Ex - ca - vat - ing for a mine,

                                     D⇨   **A⁷**⇨
Dwelt a min - er, for - ty - nin - er, And his daugh - ter

                    D⇨
Clem - en - tine. Oh my dar - ling, oh my dar - ling, Oh my

                 A⁷⇨   **D**⇨
dar - ling Clem - en - tine, You are lost and gone for - ev - er

                A⇨   **D**⇨
Dreadful sor - ry, Clem - en - tine.

1) Straight strum until you can play the entire song without stopping the strum.

2) ⊓V ⊓V ⊓V ⊓V strum pattern.

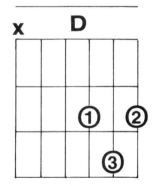

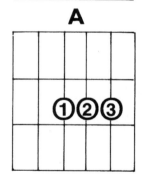

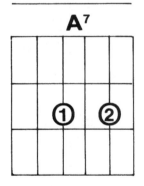

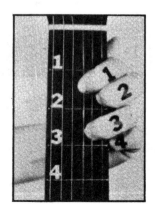

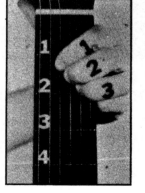

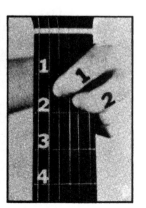

DOWN BY THE RIVERSIDE

D⇨
I'm gonna lay my sword and shield down,

A⇨   *D*⇨
Down by the riverside, down by the riverside, down by the riverside,

I'm gonna lay my sword and shield down,

A⁷⇨   *D*⇨
Down by the riverside and study war no more.

1) Straight strum until you can play the entire song without stopping the strum.

2)  strum pattern

D	A	A⁷
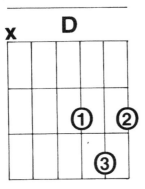	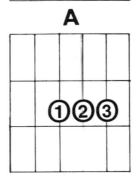	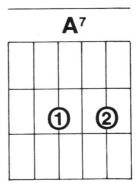
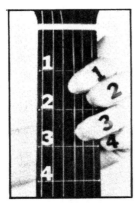	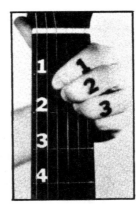	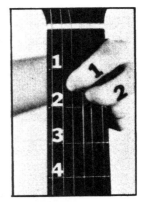

TOM DOOLEY

D⇨   *A*⇨
Met her on the hill - top, there I took her life, Met her on

                              D⇨
the hill - top, stabbed her with my knife. Hang down your head,

                              A⁷⇨
Tom Doo - ley, Hang down your head and cry, killed poor Laura

                         D⇨
Foster, you know you're bound to die.

1) Straight strum until you can play the entire song without stopping the strum.

2) ⊓V ⊓V ⊓V ⊓V strum pattern.

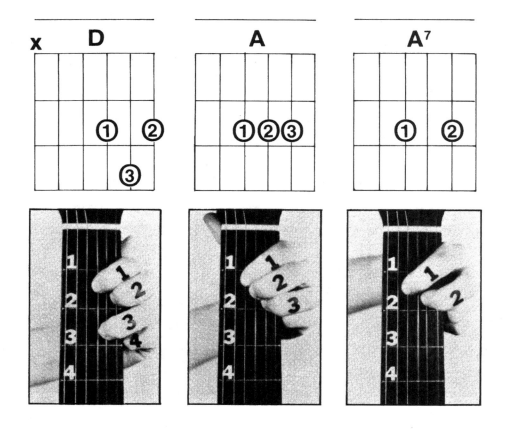

We will now go on to more advanced chords and strumming patterns.

LEARNING BY ASSOCIATION
(17 More Chords)

Learning the finger positions of 17 different chords could be quite confusing. You will be shown these **17 chords in a** way that will not only make remembering them easier, but in a **way** that **will show you how to actually move from one chord to another.**

The chords wil be presented in the order of their similarities in finger position. The similarities should help you to remember the chords and to show you the easiest way to change from one chord to another.

Am

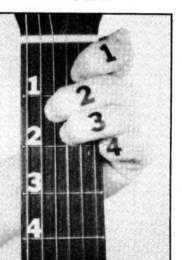

E, Am
(Chord Position And Movement)

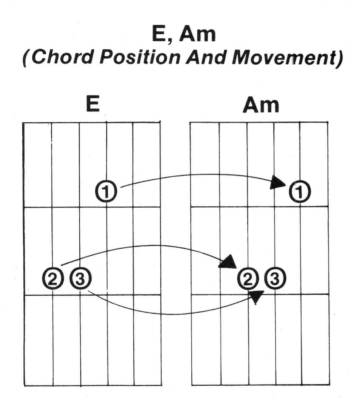

E

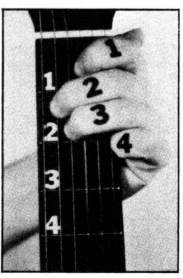

Chord Movement

Chord diagrams will be placed next to one another according to similarities in finger positions. **The arrows will show you how to change or move your fingers from one chord to another.**

Am⁷, E⁷, Em⁷ *(Chord Position And Movement)*

Am⁷

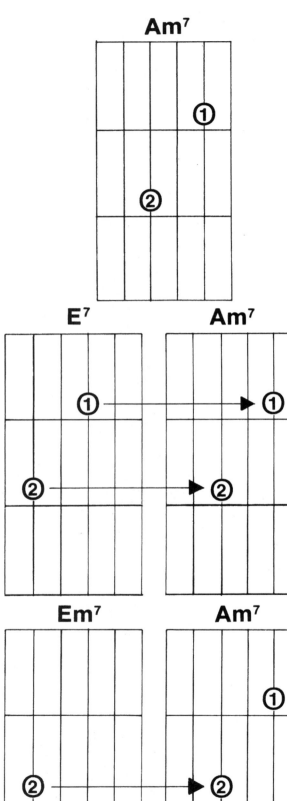

Am⁷

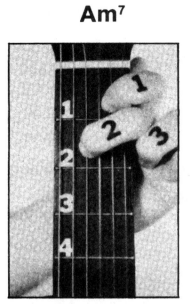

E⁷

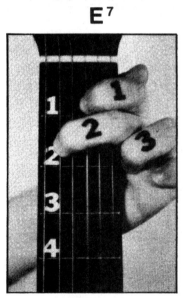

Em⁷

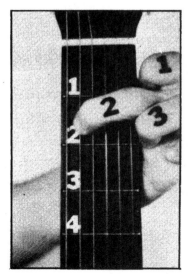

B♭m , Fmaj⁷, C *(Chord Position And Movement)*

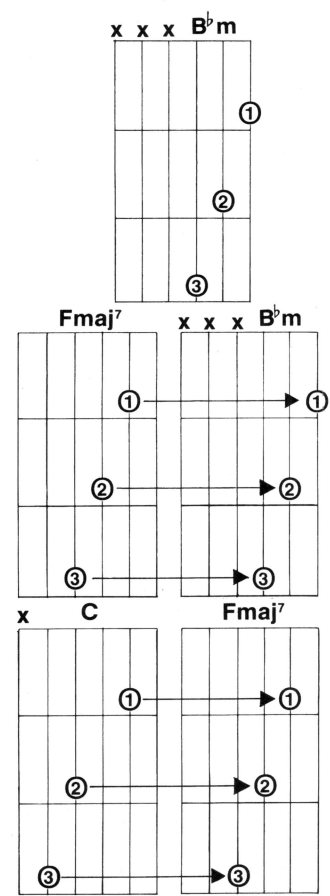

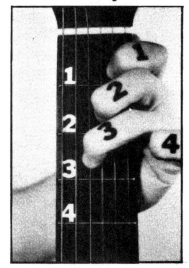

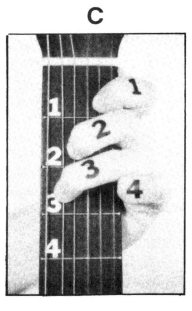

Dm, G, G⁷ *(Chord Position And Movement)*

x   **Dm**

Dm

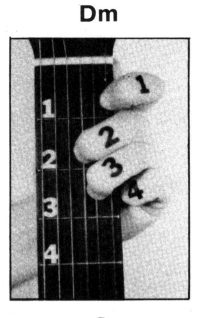

G   **x**   **Dm**

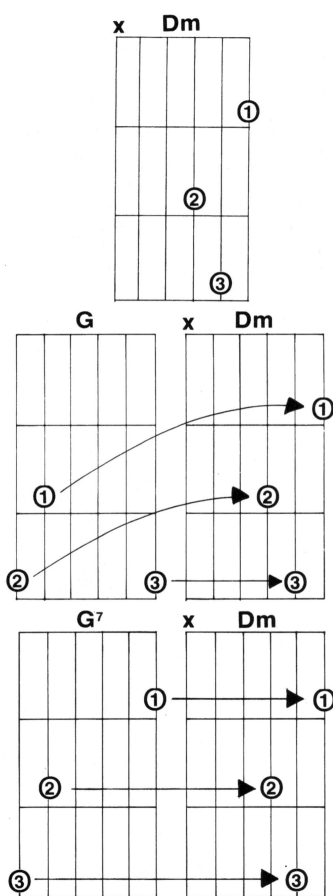

G

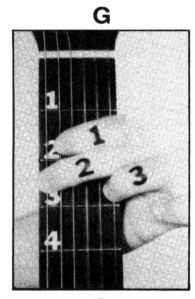

G⁷   **x**   **Dm**

G⁷

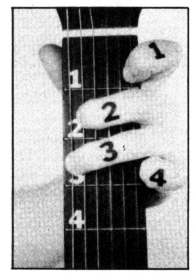

F, Dm⁷, Fm *(Chord Position And Movement)*

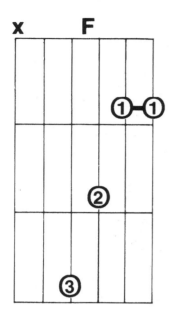

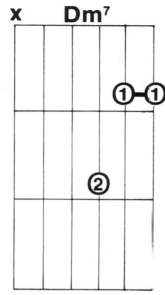

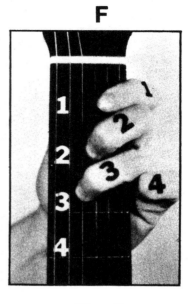

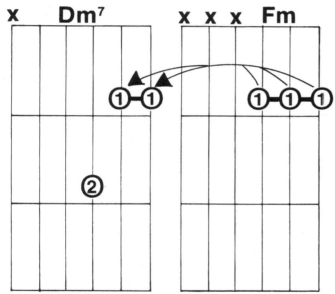

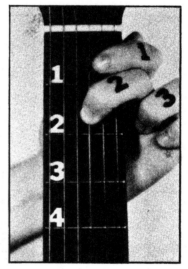

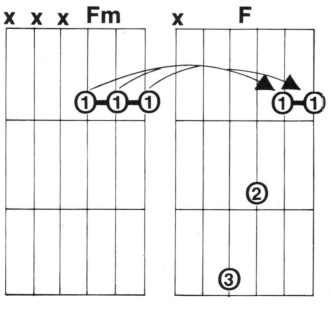

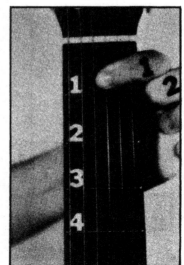

24

Em, A⁷, D⁷ *(Chord Position And Movement)*

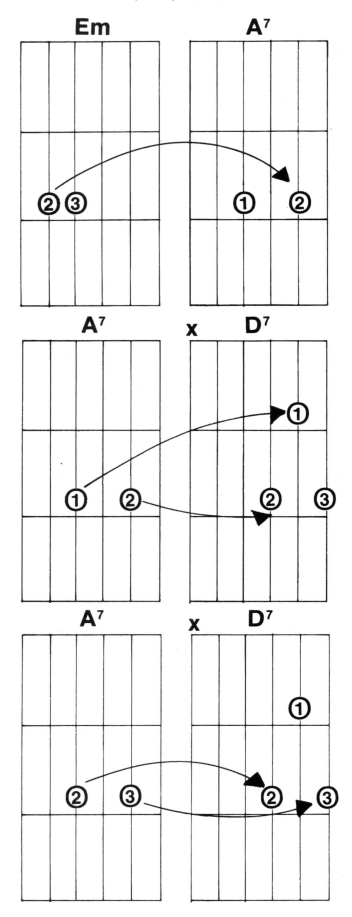

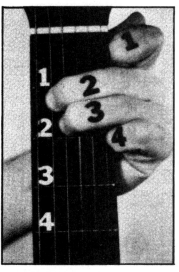

Em

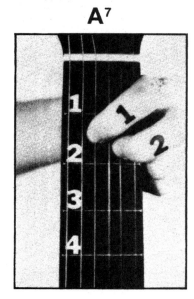

A⁷

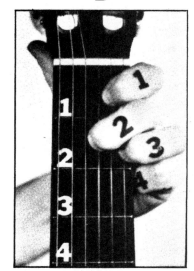

D⁷

YOUR FINGER MOVEMENT

You are probably thinking that many chords do not have similar finger positions. When changing from one chord to another you should try to keep these things in mind:

1) Often chords that do not seem to be similar often do have common fingering.

2) **You should always look** for the **easiest way** to **change from one chord to another.**

3) As you can see, in the example below your fingers should move along the strings to the next finger position with as little effort as possible.

Example

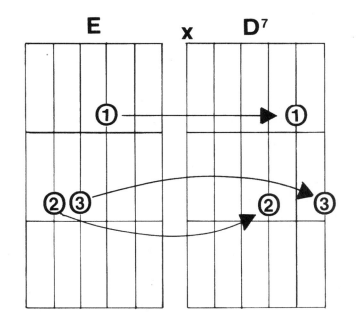

STRUM PATTERN - DOWN,DOWN,UP UP,DOWN
(⊓⊓∨∨⊓)

The strum pattern we are going to learn is ⊓⊓∨∨⊓
(down, down, up up, down).

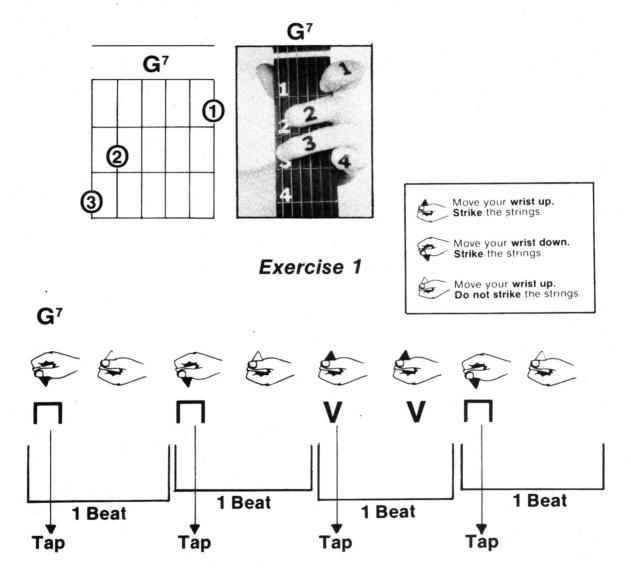

G⁷

Exercise 1

Move your **wrist up.**
Strike the strings.

Move your **wrist down.**
Strike the strings.

Move your **wrist up.**
Do not strike the strings.

G⁷

⊓   ⊓   ∨   ∨   ⊓

1 Beat   1 Beat   1 Beat   1 Beat

Tap   Tap   Tap   Tap

This exercise should be **played** in a **4 beat time period** - The time it
takes for your foot to tap the floor 4 times.

How To Change Chords Without Breaking The Strum Pattern

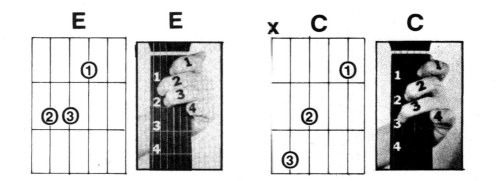

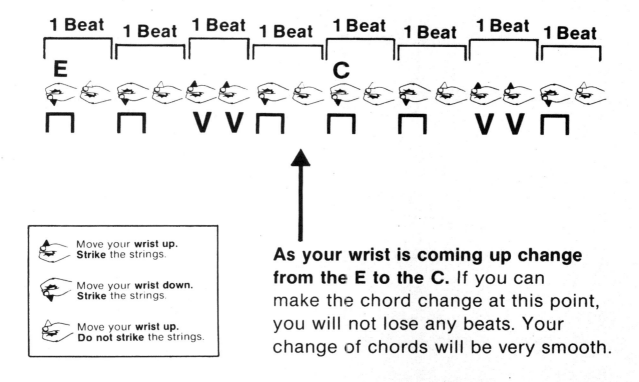

Move your **wrist up.**
Strike the strings.

Move your **wrist down.**
Strike the strings.

Move your **wrist up.**
Do not strike the strings.

As your wrist is coming up change from the E to the C. If you can make the chord change at this point, you will not lose any beats. Your change of chords will be very smooth.

1) You should make your chord change as your wrist is coming up. If you do this there will be no break in the strum pattern.

2) **You should** be able to **play** the **E and C chords** above **within** an **8 beat** or an **8 tap time period.**

ACTUAL PLAY OF SONGS (II)
KUM - BA - YAH

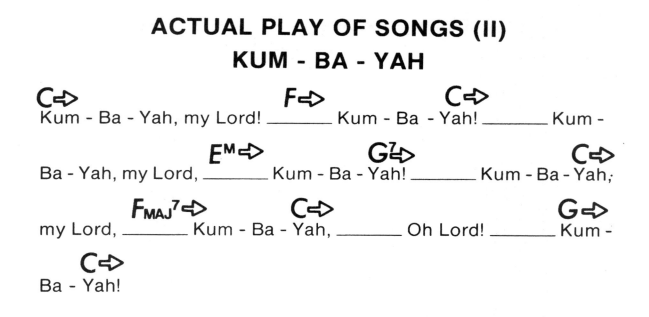

C⇨   F⇨   C⇨

Kum - Ba - Yah, my Lord! _____ Kum - Ba - Yah! _____ Kum -

E^M⇨   G^7⇨   C⇨

Ba - Yah, my Lord, _____ Kum - Ba - Yah! _____ Kum - Ba - Yah;

F$_{MAJ}$^{7}⇨   C⇨   G⇨

my Lord, _____ Kum - Ba - Yah, _____ Oh Lord! _____ Kum -

C⇨

Ba - Yah!

Helpful Advice

1) The **F** bar chord is very difficult for most people to play. Just keep practicing the **F** and eventually you will get a nice, clear sound.

2) Straight strum until you can play the entire song without stopping the strum.

3) ⊓⊓VV⊓ strum pattern.

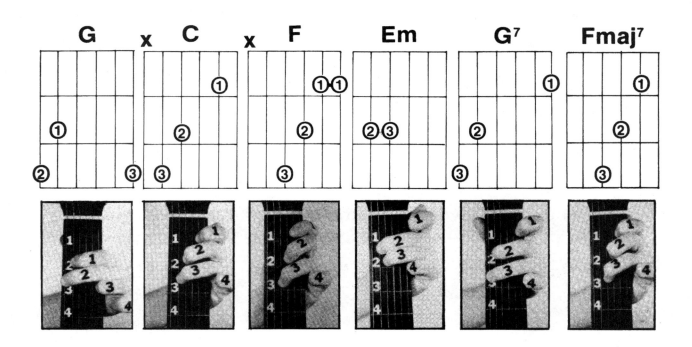

WHEN JOHNNY COMES MARCHING HOME

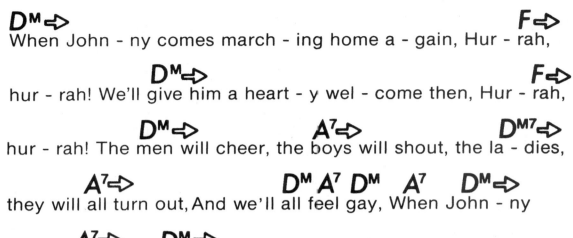

D^M⇨   F⇨
When John - ny comes march - ing home a - gain, Hur - rah,

       D^M⇨   F⇨
hur - rah! We'll give him a heart - y wel - come then, Hur - rah,

       D^M⇨   A⁷⇨   D^{M7}⇨
hur - rah! The men will cheer, the boys will shout, the la - dies,

     A⁷⇨   D^M A⁷ D^M   A⁷   D^M⇨
they will all turn out, And we'll all feel gay, When John - ny

     A⁷⇨   D^M⇨
comes marching home.

1) Straight strum until you can play the entire song without stopping the strum.

2) Try the strum pattern ⊓⊓∨⊓ down, down up, down, for this song.

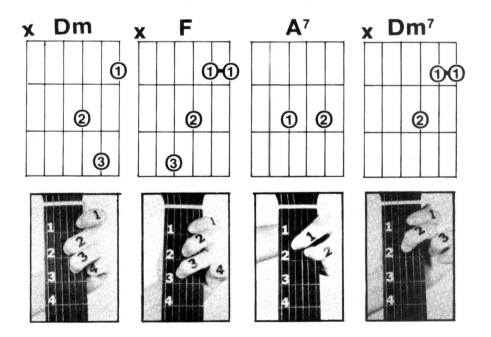

SCARBOROUGH FAIR

A^M⇨   G⇨   A^M⇨ C⇨
Oh where are you go - ing to Scar - bor - ought fair, sa -vory,

A^M⇨   C⇨   E⇨   A^M⇨   C⇨
sage, rose - ma - ry, and thyme; Re - mem - ber me to a lass

G⇨ E⇨A^M⇨   G⇨   A^M⇨
that lives there, For once she was a true love of mine.

1) Straight strum until you can play the entire song without
   stopping the strum.

2) Try the strum pattern ⊓⊓V⊓ down, down up, down,
   for this song.

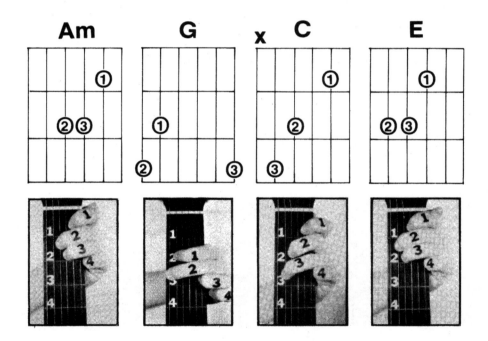

I'VE BEEN WORKING ON THE RAILROAD

C⇨   F⇨   C⇨
I've been work-ing on the rail - road, All the live long day

C⇨   D⁷⇨   G⇨
I've been working on the rail - road, Just to pass the time a - way

G⇨   C⇨   F⇨   E⁷⇨
Don't you hear the whis-tle blow - ing, Rise up so ear-ly in the morn;

F⇨   C⇨   G⇨   C
Can't you hear the cap-tain shout in' __ Din - ah blow your horn.

1) Straight strum until you can play the entire song without stopping the strum.

2) ⊓⊓∨∨⊓ strum pattern.

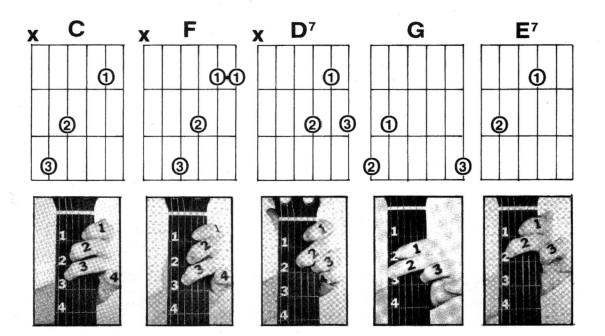

LEARNING BY ASSOCIATION
(11 More Chords)

We will now present 11 more chords. They will be grouped according to their similarities in finger positions. These chords are quite difficult since they involve the use of your 4th finger while also using your bar positions. (A bar chord is a chord in which you press 2 or more strings down with the same finger.)

B⁷, B♭
(Chord Position And Movement)

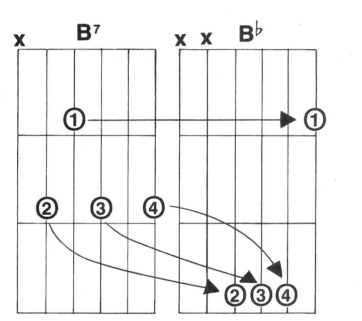

Try fingering the 11 chords in this section.

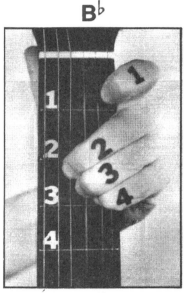

B♭

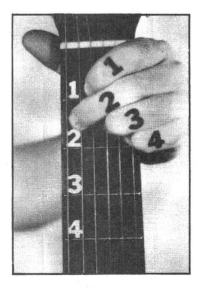

B⁷

C⁷, C#dim, Cm *(Chord Position And Movement)*

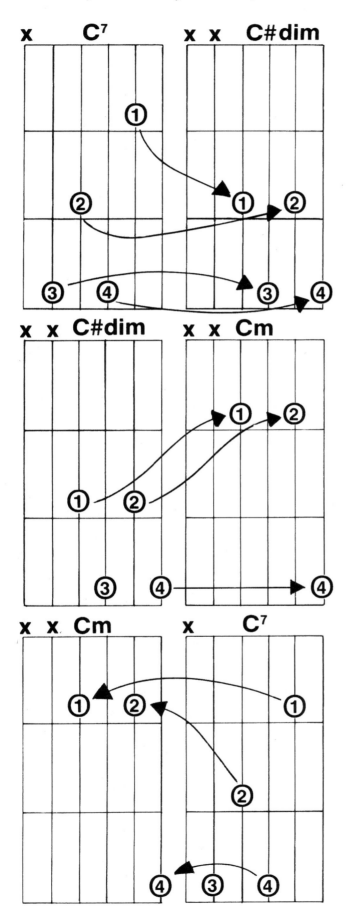

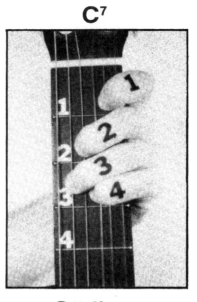

C⁷

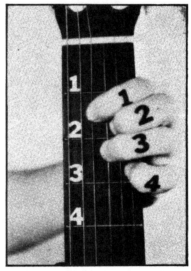

C#dim

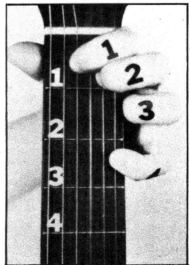

Cm

F⁷, F⁶, F⁹ *(Chord Position And Movement)*

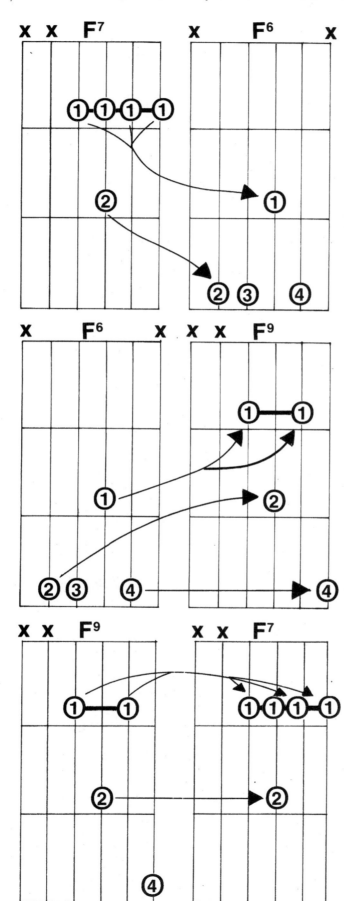

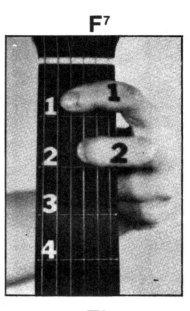

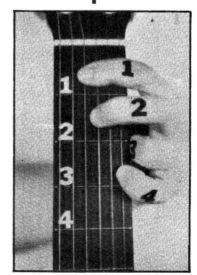

Gm⁷, Fm⁷, Gm *(Chord Position And Movement)*

x x **Gm⁷**

③-③-③-③

x x **Fm⁷**

①-①-①-①

Gm⁷

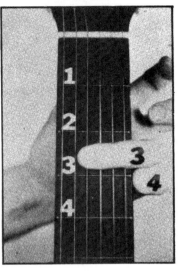

x x **Fm⁷**

①-①-①-①

x x **Gm⁷**

③-③-③-③

Fm⁷

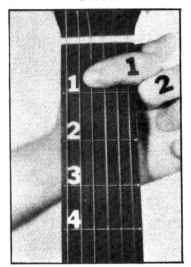

x x **Gm**

③-③-③

x x **Fm⁷**

①-①-①-①

Gm

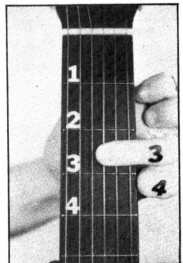

STRUM PATTERN
DOWN, DOWN UP, DOWN, DOWN
(⊓⊓V⊓⊓)

The strum we will be using is
(Down, Down Up, Down, Down)

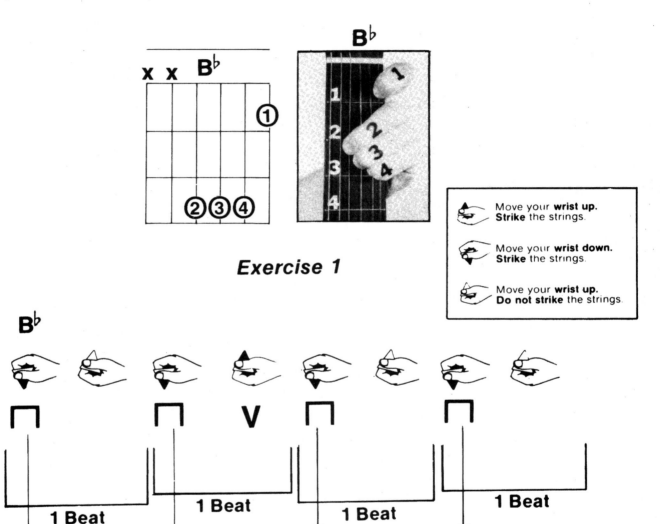

Exercise 1

1) **This exercise** should be **played** in a **4 beat time span.**

2) You should be able to play this exercise in the same time it takes to tap your foot 4 times.

How To Change Chords Without Breaking The Strum Pattern

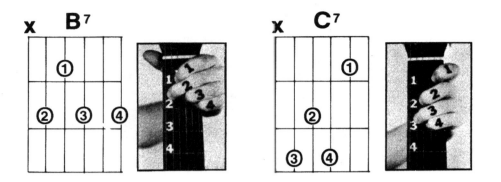

Exercise 2

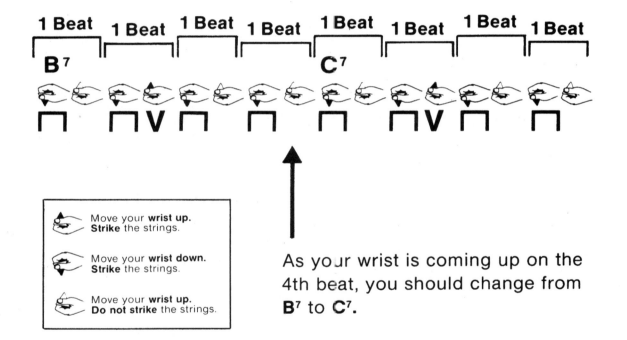

	Move your **wrist up.** **Strike** the strings.
	Move your **wrist down.** **Strike** the strings.
	Move your **wrist up.** **Do not strike** the strings.

As your wrist is coming up on the 4th beat, you should change from **B⁷** to **C⁷**.

1) **If you** can **change** the **chord as your wrist** is **coming up, there will be no break** in the **strum pattern.**

2) You should be able to play the strum pattern above using the **B⁷** and **C⁷** chords in an 8 beat time span.

3) Now try this strum with some of the 11 new chords in the following songs.

ACTUAL PLAY OF SONGS (III)
COMIN' ROUND THE MOUNTAIN

B^b ⇨
She'll be com - in' round the moun - tain when she comes, she'll

F^7 ⇨
be com - in' round the moun - tain when she comes, she'll be

B^b ⇨ E^b ⇨
com - in' round the moun - tain, she'll be com - in' round the

F^7 ⇨
moun - tain, she'll be com - in' round the moun - tain when

B^b
she comes.

Helpful Advice

1) These chords are difficult for most people. **Take these three chords** and **go through the 4 steps you have just learned in the book.** You then should be able to play this song or any song, using these kind of chords.

2) Straight strum until you can play the entire song without stopping the strum.

3) ⊓⊓V⊓⊓ strum pattern.

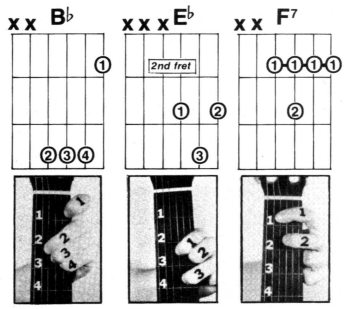

AULD LANG SYNE

B^b ⇨ F^7 ⇨ B^b ⇨
Should auld ac - quaint - ance be for - got, And nev - er

E^b ⇨ B^b ⇨ F^7 ⇨
brought to mind? Should auld ac - quaint - ance be for -

E^b ⇨ B^b ⇨ F^7 ⇨
got, And days of auld lang syne? For auld - lang syne,

B^b ⇨ E^b ⇨ B^b ⇨
my dear, For auld - lang - syne; We'll take a cup o'

F^7 ⇨ E^b ⇨ B^b
kind - ness yet For auld - lang - syne.

1) Straight strum until you can play the entire song without stopping the strum.

2) ⊓⊓V⊓⊓ strum pattern.

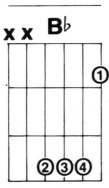

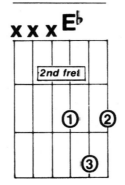

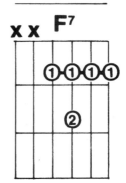

HAVA NAGILAH

G ⇨
Ha - va _____ Na - gi - lah,   Ha - va _____ Na - gi - lah,

Cᴹ ⇨   **G** ⇨
Ha - va _____ Na - gi - lah,   vay - nis _____ m' chayh,

G ⇨
Ha - va _____ Na - gi - lah   Ha - va _____ Na - gi - lah,

Cᴹ ⇨   **G** ⇨
Ha - va _____ Na - gi - lah,   vay - nis _____ m' chayh.

G ⇨   **F**ᴹ ⇨
Hav - a n' ra - ne - nah, ha - va n' ra - ne - nah,

Fᴹ ⇨   **G** ⇨
Ha - va n' ra - ne - nah, vay - nis _____ m' - chayh. Ha - va n'

                    Fᴹ ⇨
ra - ne - nah, ha - va n' - ra - ne - nah, ha - va n' - ra - ne - nah,

G ⇨
vay - nis _____ m' - chayh.

1) Straight strum until you can play the entire song without stopping the strum.

2) ⊓⊓V⊓⊓ strum pattern.

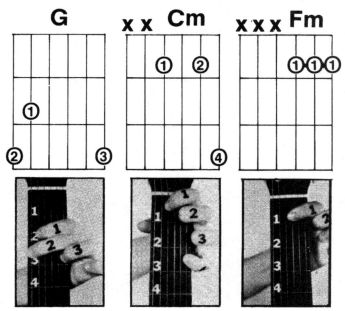

BEAUTIFUL DREAMER

B^b ⇨ C^M ⇨ F^7 ⇨

Beau - ti - ful dream - er, wake un - to me. Star - light

                    B^b ⇨

and dew drops are wait - ing for thee; Sounds of the rude

C^M ⇨ F^7 ⇨

world heard in the day. Lulled by the moon - light have

    B^b ⇨ F^7 ⇨ B^b ⇨

all passed a - way! Beau -ti - ful dream - er, queen

       C^M ⇨ F^7 ⇨

of my song, list while I woo thee with soft mel - o - dy;

B^b ⇨ C^M ⇨ F^7 ⇨

Gone are the cares of life's bus - y throng, Beau - ti - ful

      B^b ⇨

dream - er a - wake un - to me.

1) Straight strum until you can play the entire song **without** stopping the strum.

2) Try the strum pattern ⊓⊓V⊓ down, down up, down for this song.

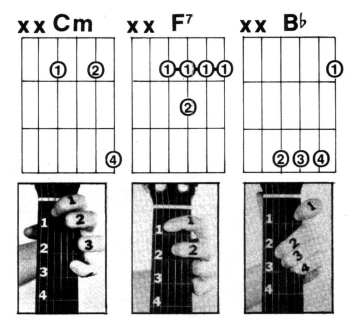

xx Cm   xx F⁷   xx B♭

USING A CAPO (CĀPŌ)

A Capo

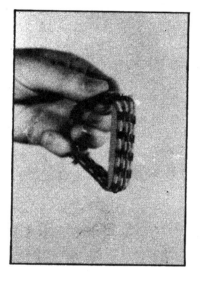

Placing A Capo On The Guitar

The capo should be placed directly above the fret line.

Why A Capo Is Used

A capo is used to raise the chords or the key of a song. By **using a capo you can raise the key** of a song **to accomodate your voice.** The capo automatically changes the names of the chord forms being used.

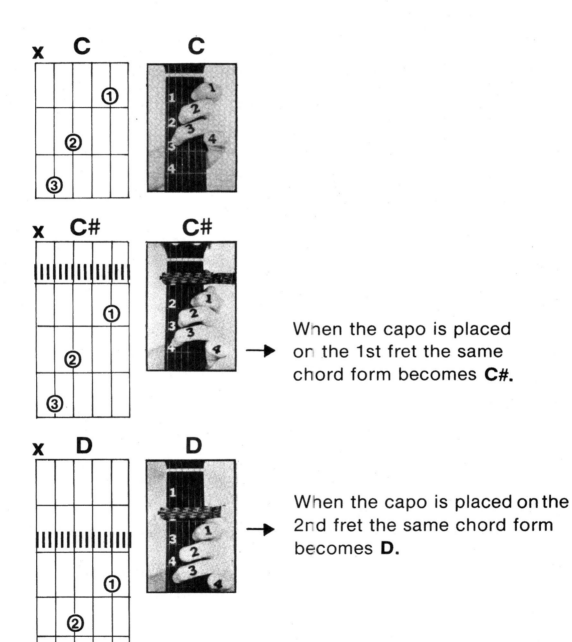

When the capo is placed on the 1st fret the same chord form becomes **C#.**

When the capo is placed on the 2nd fret the same chord form becomes **D.**

The Capo Chart

With the chart below you can change one chord form into a variety of chords.

Basic Chord Names	A#/Bb	B	C	C#/Db	D	D#/Eb	E	F	F#/Gb	G	G#/Ab	A
Capo placed on 1st fret	B	C	C#/Db	D	D#/Eb	E	F	F#/Gb	G	G#/Ab	A	A#/Bb
Capo placed on 2nd fret	C	C#/Db	D	D#/Eb	E	F	F#/Gb	G	G#/Ab	A	A#/Bb	B
Capo placed on 3rd fret	C#/Db	D	D#/Eb	E	F	F#/Gb	G	G#/Ab	A	A#/Bb	B	C
Capo placed on 4th fret	D	D#/Eb	E	F	F#/Gb	G	G#/Ab	A	A#/Bb	B	C	C#/Db
Capo placed on 5th fret	D#/Eb	E	F	F#/Gb	G	G#/Ab	A	A#/Bb	B	C	C#/Db	D
Capo placed on 6th fret	E	F	F#/Gb	G	G#/Ab	A	A#/Bb	B	C	C#/Db	D	D#/Eb
Capo placed on 7th fret	F	F#/Gb	G	G#/Ab	A	A#/Bb	B	C	C#/Db	D	D#/Eb	E
Capo placed on 8th fret	F#/Gb	G	G#/Ab	A	A#/Bb	B	C	C#/Db	D	D#/Eb	E	F
Capo placed on 9th fret	G	G#/Ab	A	A#/Bb	B	C	C#/Db	D	D#/Eb	E	F	F#/Gb
Capo placed on 10th fret	G#/Ab	A	A#/Bb	B	C	C#/Db	D	D#/Eb	E	F	F#/Gb	G

The capo changes the chord's letter name only. In other words, if your chord was Dm (1st position Dm and you placed the capo on the 1st fret the chord becomes D#m). The letter name is changed from D to D#, however the chord remains a minor chord. If you started out with a F#dim chord (1st position F#dim) and placed the capo on the 4th fret, the chord would become A#dim. Again, the chords letter name (1st row in your chart) F# is changed to A# but the chord remains a diminished chord.

How To Use The Capo Chart

The easiest way to use the capo and the capo chart is to always find the 1st position chord. A 1st postion chord is the chord form that is played on the 1st three frets of guitar.

Example - Capo Chart And A Song

(A) 1) Let us say that the chords of your song are **Am, E⁷, and C.**

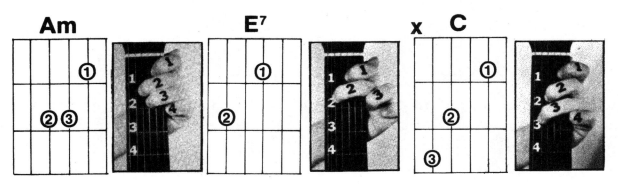

2) You would like to make the song slightly higher. You place the capo across the first fret.

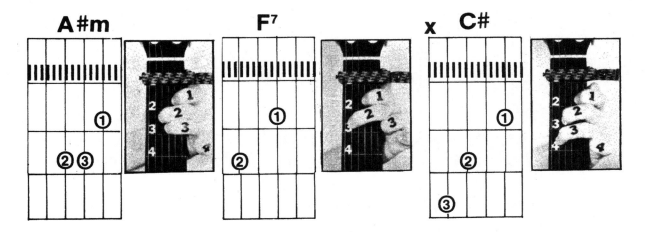

Checking your capo chart you can see that **Am** would become **A#m, E⁷** would be **F⁷** and **C** would become **C#.** Remember, you would still have the same song and be using the same chord forms, but the song would be slightly higher.

How To Use The Capo Chart

(B) 1)   Let us say that the chord form begins on the 2nd fret. To get the correct chord form you must move the chord form down one fret.

Example 1

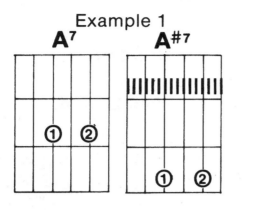

A⁷   A#⁷

Example 2

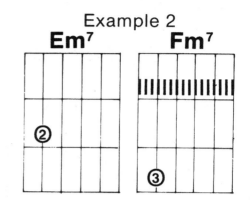

Em⁷   Fm⁷

(C)   If you are using a 1st position bar chord that begins on the 1st fret, you would simply remove the bar with your finger when placing the capo on the 1st fret.

Example 1   Example 2

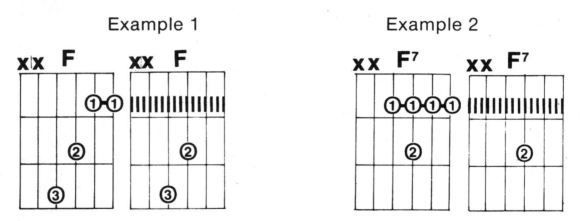

1) Let us say that the chord form begins on the 2nd fret. To get the correct chord form you must move the chord form down one fret.

   If you are using a 1st position bar chord that begins on the 1st fret, you would simply remove the bar with your finger when placing the capo on the 1st fret.

1) **As you can see bar chords that begin on the first fret would retain their same name when the capo is placed on the guitar. The capo chart will not work for these chords.**

2) Strings that are not played (as x's on the diagrams indicate) on the 1st position chords would not be played when the capo is placed on the guitar.

HOW TO MAKE UP YOUR OWN STRUM

You must remember the beats when you are strumming your guitar. Each strumming pattern you make up should be played with a 2, 3, or 4 beat span.

Time Signature

The **amount of beats** in the **strum pattern** are **given to you** at the beginning of a song **by means of a time signature.**

This song has 4 beats per measure. (4 beat strum pattern)

This time signature is the same as a $\frac{4}{4}$ time signature requiring a 4 beat strum pattern.

This song has a 3 beat strum pattern.

This song has a 2 beat strum pattern.

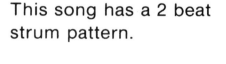

1) As you have seen from the various songs we have completed so far, the number of strums does not necessarily equal the number of beats.

Example

1) 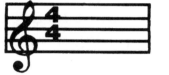 strum equals one beat.
2) **V V** strum equals one beat.

2) The time signature tells you the number of beats you should have in your strum pattern.

Example  This time signature would have 4 beat strum patterns.

Possible strum patterns (4 beats)

4 beats = **4 beats** = **4 beats**

Any of the **above strum patterns** could be played because they **all are done in 4 beats.**

3) Let us say the song has a [time signature image] time signature.

This time signature indicates that there are 3 beats per measure. You would have to create a 3 beat strum pattern.

Example

3 beats = **3 beats** = **3 beats**

Any of the **above strum patterns** can be **done in 3 beats.**

Conclusion

1) Look at the time signature to see how many beats are required in your strum pattern.

2) Your strum pattern could be any combination or pattern of strums as long as it can be done in the number of beats required in the time signature.

3) Your strum pattern should remain the same throughout the song.

4) The speed of the strum pattern depends on the speed of the song.

5) **Good luck and happy strumming.**

Student Notes